Introducing
EUROPEAN COSTUME

Glasgow Museums

First published in 2015 by Glasgow Museums to accompany the exhibition *A Century of Style: Costume and Colour 1800–1899* at Kelvingrove Art Gallery and Museum 25 September 2015–14 February 2016. All rights reserved. No part of this publication may be reproduced or transmitted in any form or by any means, electronic or mechanical, including photocopying, recording, or any other information storage and retrieval system, without prior permission in writing from the publisher.

ISBN 978-1-908638-25-0

British Library Cataloguing in Publication Data

A catalogue record for this book is available from the British Library

p.62 © Reproduced by kind permission of Judith Witts
p.63 © The Stewartry Museum, Kirkcudbright

Written by Rebecca Quinton
Designed by Fiona MacDonald
Edited by Fiona MacLeod
Photography by Enzo di Cosmo, Ellen Howden and Jim Dunn
Printed in Scotland by Allander

Acknowledgments

Thanks to Jade Halbert and Emma Morrison for editorial assistance.

Front cover image:
Detail of dress by Jeanne Lanvin
E.1978.86

Introducing
EUROPEAN COSTUME

Rebecca Quinton

R. Simpson & Sons.
COSTUMIERS
JAMAICA ST. CORNER
Glasgow

Jeanne Lanvin
PARIS
UNIS FRANCE

34/36
Cashmere
by
Pringle
BY APPOINTMENT TO H.M. THE QUEEN MANUFACTURERS OF KNITTED GARMENTS MADE IN

STYLED BY Pringle FOR
Dalys OF GLASGOW
MADE IN SCOTLAND

Mess. Hayward
Court Dressmakers
04 New Bond Str.
LONDON W.

Hallmark
ISLAND PARADISE
Size: LARGE 16-18   395.PD84-4
80% Cellulose 20% Cotton
This fabric is fire-resistant, however — fabric will be
dangerously flammable if dry-cleaned or washed.
Hallmark Cards, Inc.   Kansas City, Missouri   Made in U.S.A.

ROBES & CONFECTIONS
MERLOT LARCHEVÊQUE
23, BOULEVART DES CAPUCINES, 23

John Bates
LONDON

J. MACNEILLE
BOOT & SHOE
Maker
AYR

Contents

FOREWORD

2015 is an exciting time for the European Costume collection in Glasgow Museums, with our first major exhibition in over 20 years. With new displays, publications and improved digital provision, the European Costume and Textiles collection will become fully accessible to the public. Long-term aspirations include developing the collection – in particular post-1970s fashion – to better reflect the style of Glasgow and its people past and present, and to inspire new generations of designers and enthusiasts.

Introducing European Costume gives the first overview of the historic European Costume collection in Glasgow Museums. It offers a snapshot of our star pieces after over 100 years of collecting. Some may be familiar to regular visitors to our venues, such as Kelvingrove Art Gallery & Museum and Riverside Museum. Others are being introduced for the first time. Research on the collection is constantly being undertaken by the curatorial staff, assisted in recent years by students on the MLitt Art History: Dress and Textile Histories course at the University of Glasgow.

This book has been published to mark the occasion of the first major costume exhibition from our collection since 1992. *A Century of Style: Costume & Colour 1800–1899* showcases some of the best examples of nineteenth-century dress, while this book spans items of early seventeenth-century costume which are currently on display in the Burrell Collection through to items from the twentieth century on view at Riverside Museum.

Conservation has a major role in preparing items safely for display. Costume conservation and mounting requires an understanding of how clothes were cut at the time of their manufacture and the techniques that were used in their construction. No less important is a knowledge of what undergarments were worn, as these can have a direct effect on the appearance and profile of the costume on a mannequin.

The correct profile of a costume is dependent on preparing the mannequin with underpinnings of the right period. These replica garments are made by taking patterns of original items, including corsets, bustles and crinolines, and replicating them using modern materials. This work is time consuming but essential to provide adequate support for the costume while on display.

Occasionally costumes are incomplete and replica items are made using modern materials, following original patterns where possible. The exhibition and display of costume involves conservators, curators, designers, photographers and technicians, but it is our great privilege to breathe life back into these wonderful garments once more.

Duncan Dornan,
Head of Museums and Collections, Glasgow Life

Textile conservator Maggie
Dobbie preparing an accessory in
the Textile Conservation Studio.

INTRODUCTION

Glasgow Museums started collecting European costume in the 1870s. Some early donations were from now defunct local manufacturers, such as Turkey Red handkerchiefs made by Archibald Orr Ewing & Co. They reflect the major textile industries – including carpet production and calico printing – of the city and surrounding area that flourished during the late 1800s. Items made in continental Europe, purchased from the Glasgow International Exhibition in 1888, were soon added to the collection with the aim of providing sources of inspiration for local design companies.

The collection continued to develop during the early decades of the twentieth century, mainly as a result of generous gifts from the public that ranged from individual pieces to collections of family heirlooms. Some notable donations include 1780s'–1840s' costume worn by the Houstons of Johnstone Castle and a large group of accessories from Miss Fernanda Jacobsen, many of which were presented to her when she was Commandant of the Scottish Ambulance Unit during the Spanish Civil War. The reliance on donations initially resulted in a random and disparate collection. However, the appointment of the first specialist curator in the 1970s led to a more systematic approach to collecting that continues today, helped by the occasional purchase of key items.

There are several areas of strength in the collection. Exquisitely embroidered costume from the early 1600s forms part of the internationally significant gift of Sir William Burrell. The collection of eighteenth-century costume, whilst not particularly large, contains a number of items with Scottish provenances including a rare example of a tartan coat from the 1740s. There is a strong collection of late 1800s' womenswear, with a number of high quality garments made by Glasgow's leading department stores and dressmakers.

Due to the growth in mass-production during the twentieth century it is not surprising that clothes from that period form the largest part of the collection. Whilst there are examples of internationally important designers, the focus is on Glasgow-based designers, manufacturers and wearers, most notably alumni of The Glasgow School of Art.

Glasgow Museums also holds some thematic collections, particularly sports and leisurewear, which has grown in importance in recent years as Glasgow has hosted a number of major international sporting events, including the XX Commonwealth Games in 2014. Meanwhile, the creative side of the city, which is home to many of Scotland's national arts organizations, is represented by a growing number of performance costumes.

17th

Seventeenth-
century
costume

Fashionable life during the 1600s revolved around the Royal Courts of Europe. In Britain the Union of the Crowns in 1603, when James VI of Scotland inherited the English throne after the death of Elizabeth I, led to a period of peace and prosperity.

Jacobean courtiers dressed in extravagant embroidered garments that demonstrated their wealth and position in society. The end of sumptuary laws, that had restricted the use of expensive textiles to nobility, meant that rich merchants and professionals could wear fashionable clothing too. Gentlemen wore doublets and breeches accessorized with feather hats, short capes and embroidered gloves. Ladies dressed in full-length gowns or waistcoats over skirts, known as petticoats. Both male and female outfits were completed with delicate white needle- or bobbin-lace collars and cuffs. In the late 1620s taste was led by Charles I and his French wife, Henrietta Maria, who brought in fashions from the court of her brother, Louis XIII of France. Waistlines were raised and sumptuous silk satins were decorated with slashed, stamped or pinked patterns.

The Civil Wars influenced dress during the middle of the century. Whilst there were those on both sides who wore flamboyant Cavalier styles, there were religious groups, such as the Puritans, who favoured a more sombre look of crisp white lace and linen worn over contrasting black garments – a look that

'…Gentlemen's doublets were cut short and trimmed with yards of ribbons…'

sometimes could be just as costly to manufacture as the more colourful outfits. The Restoration of Charles II in 1660 from his exile in Europe introduced the latest continental fashions from Louis XIV's new court at Versailles. Gentlemen's doublets were cut short and trimmed with yards of ribbons, whilst in contrast ladies' gowns were constructed with long, boned bodices. However, within a few years Charles II introduced a new form of garment, the Persian vest, which would by the end of the century evolve into the forerunner of the three-piece suit.

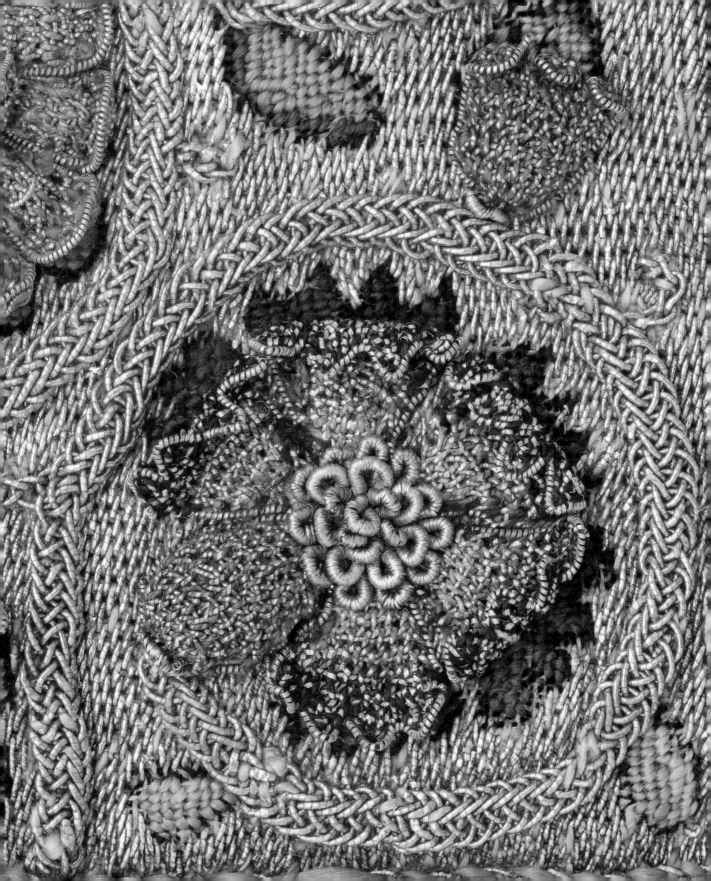

Sweet bag, 1600–30
Bought by the Burrell Trustees, 1991
29.310

There were several uses for small
embroidered sweet bags. Some were
filled with scented potpourri and stored
in clothes chests. Others contained small
prayer books or sewing accessories to be
worn suspended from a girdle around
the waist. The most lavish examples
were given as presents on important
occasions, such as New Year, filled with
money or jewels.

Facing page:
Waistcoat, about 1615–18
Gifted as part of the Burrell Collection to the City of
Glasgow, 1944
29.127

Long-sleeved waistcoats of embroidered linen were worn
by wealthy ladies in the early 1600s. Patterns with brightly-
coloured flowers and insects set within gilt coils were very
popular during this period. The embroidery was stitched
first by professionals and then the panels were sewn
together to form the waistcoat, with any adjustments to
fit made at the back. Delicate white lace collar and cuffs, a
long gown worn open at the front and an embroidered silk
petticoat would have completed the outfit.

Petticoat

This is a very rare petticoat from the court of Anne of Denmark, Queen Consort of James VI of Scotland and I of England. Petticoats were worn with waistcoats as a more informal option to a gown.

The vibrant crimson red silk satin was probably dyed using an expensive imported insect dye, such as cochineal. The embroidered border of scrolling stems surrounding colourful flowers, including honeysuckle, pinks, lilies, roses and thistles is worked in silk and metal threads. There are also various fruit, birds, butterflies and other insects, as well as miniature raised and padded hearts.

Small ermine tail motifs cover the centre and reflect the aristocratic status of the wearer, who wore the petticoat arranged over a hooped farthingale or padded roll tied around the hips. The ends were left open at the centre front to reveal a forepart panel.

The petticoat is said to have been given by Anne's son, Charles I, to one of his most loyal servants, William Levett, Page of the Backstairs and later Groom of the Bedchamber. It passed down through his wife's family, and several alterations and repairs were made over the subsequent centuries.

Petticoat, about 1610–20
Bought by the Burrell Trustees with the assistance of the Art Fund, 1996
29.314

17

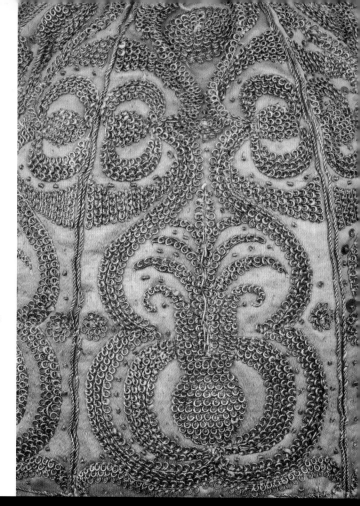

Nightcap and slippers, about 1640–60
Gifted as part of the Burrell Collection to
the City of Glasgow, 1944
29.133, 29.144–145

These accessories, together with the waistcoat opposite, are
said to have belonged to Charles II, when Prince of Wales.
The delicate pink silk satin is decorated with silver and
silver-gilt threads laid and couched in place. The motif may
be a stylized pineapple, which was introduced to Europe
by Christopher Columbus in 1493. Charles was appointed
General of the Western Association in 1645 and is said to
have given these items to Thomas Veel of Alveston, near
Bristol, who fought with the Royalist army.

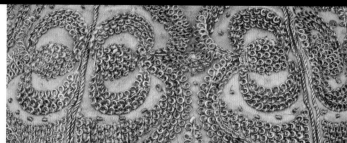

Waistcoat, about 1640–80
Gifted as part of the Burrell Collection
to the City of Glasgow, 1944
29.128

This waistcoat is made of silk satin with
a wool interlining and linen lining that
has been hand-quilted with a chevron
design. James Master's Expense Book
for 1649–50 records that he spent
£1.13.0 'for three yds of watchet
satting to make me a waistcoat'. The
waistcoat may have been made to
be worn under a buff-coat to provide
additional warmth to the wearer whilst
on campaign.

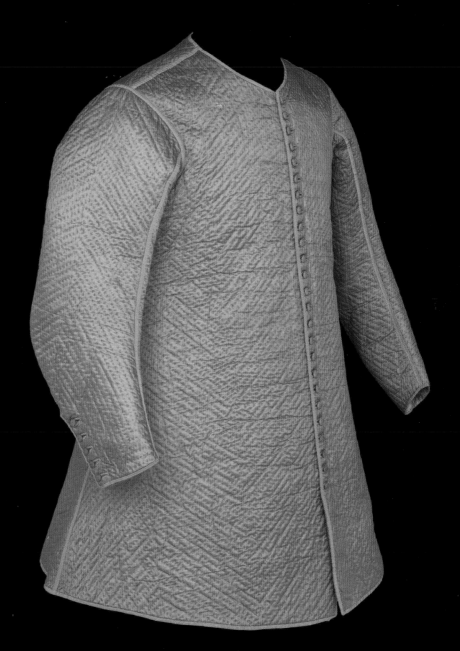

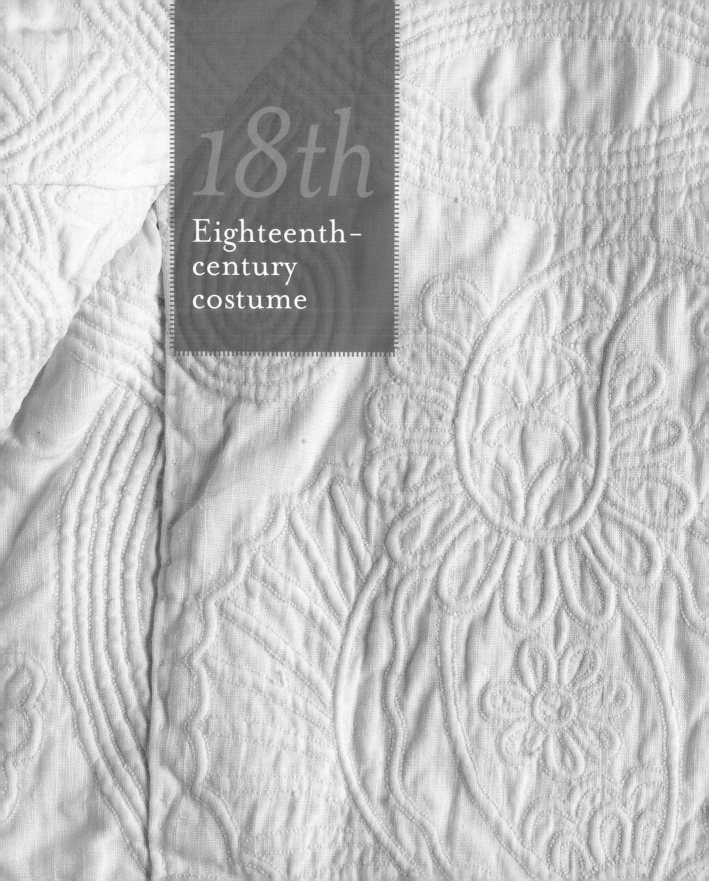

18th

Eighteenth-century costume

The Acts of Union in 1706 and 1707 created Great Britain. The joining of Scotland and England gave rise to a period of intense growth for the economy, supported by the technological advancements of the industrial revolution. This led to a huge increase in the consumption of material goods, including fashionable clothing, not only by rich aristocrats, but also by a growing number of wealthy middle-class families.

Menswear during the 1700s was dominated by matching or co-ordinating coats, waistcoats and breeches. Changing styles were reflected by the use of different fabrics and alterations to the cut of the garments, with the wide cuffs and full skirts of the

'...Changing styles were reflected by the use of different fabrics...'

early century slowly evolving into tight-fitting sleeves and narrow tails. In the early 1700s ladies wore mantuas that were worn open with a contrasting triangular stomacher at the front of the bodice and the skirts folded back to reveal the petticoat. During the 1740s the *robe à la Française* (French gown), also known as the sack-back gown, with its luxurious use of lengths of fabric falling from double-box pleats at the back, dominated women's dress. Annual fashions were observed in the introduction of new textile designs and details in the robings that trimmed the front of the gown; horizontal pleats were replaced by serpentine lines that gave way to vertically padded bands.

Formal dress for both sexes was dominated by French styles emanating from the court at Versailles. However, during the second half of the century fashionable taste both at home and on the continent was influenced by a more informal English style. Gentlemen wore wool broadcloth coats, generally reserving their French-style embroidered silks for evening wear, whilst ladies adopted the *robe à l'Anglaise* (English gown). When cotton became increasingly popular during the 1780s a new form of gown took advantage of the soft, draping nature of the fabric. Known initially as the *robe à la Reine* (Queen's gown), named after Marie Antoinette, Queen of France, this round gown with closed bodice and skirt continued in favour throughout the 1790s.

Coat

This coat is made from hard tartan – a worsted fabric that is not finished and softened, but cut straight from the loom to retain its stiffness. The individual coat pieces were carefully worked out so that the pattern or sett carefully lined up when they were sewn together to form the finished garment. The deep cuffs follow the cut of fashionable continental men's coats; however, the skirts are shorter to allow it to be worn with the Scottish *féileadh-mór* or belted plaid.

After the failure of the Jacobite Rebellion led by Prince Charles Stuart in 1746, the Hanoverian government banned the wearing of Highland dress and tartan for the majority of men living in Scotland. As a result very few pieces from this period survive. The law was repealed in 1782 and tartan enjoyed a major revival in the 1800s.

During the Victorian period it was believed that this coat was worn by a rider in Bonnie Prince Charlie's army at the Battle of Culloden in 1745. It was exhibited as such in Edinburgh in 1889 and the sett was used as the basis for the Culloden tartan in Donald William Stewart's *Old and Rare Scottish Tartans* (1893).

Coat, about 1740–45
Given by Dr JM Hendry, 1990
E.1990.59.1

'...it was
believed that
this coat
was worn
by a rider
in Bonnie
Prince
Charlie's
army ...'

Purse, about 1740–60
Given by Miss Florda D Lockhart, 1943
E.1943.71.a

This little purse is made with approximately 40,000 tiny glass beads, each individually stitched into place. The finest purses of this technique, known as *sable*, were made in France. Each of the four quarters depicts a flower; either a red rose or a blue pansy.

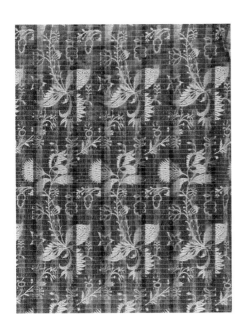

English gown, about 1770–80
Bought by Glasgow Museums, 1976
E.1976.79.1

This pretty silk is a tobine – a warp woven fabric – that has flowers woven in the pink and blue vertical warp threads, rather than the more customary horizontal weft threads. While the cut of this English gown dates to the 1770s, careful inspection reveals that it has been altered from an earlier sack-back gown of the 1750s. Remaking dresses was common in the 1700s, when expensive silks gowns were often handed down to children or passed on to ladies' maids to re-use or sell.

Waistcoat, about 1760–70
Bought by Glasgow Museums, 1917
1917.10

Fashionable gentlemen wore embroidered silk waistcoats with their dress suits on formal occasions. The small metal sequins and faceted glass pieces backed with foil and surrounded by coiled metal thread would have twinkled in the candlelight. Whilst often waistcoats were embroidered by amateur needlewomen for male relations, the quality of the stitching on this suggests it may have been made in a professional workshop.

Waistcoat, about 1770–80

Given by RG Macleod Dalven
TEMP.15667

Embroidered waistcoats from the 1700s
were sometimes kept and worn as vintage
pieces by later generations. This waistcoat
was re-used in the 1920s, but by a larger
gentleman who had panels inserted
into the side seams that have since been
removed. The dressmaker who made the
alterations left a pencil note inside one panel
stating that it 'was let out by Mrs Hastie 9
Johnstone St Paisley 15.6.22. for Captain
McArthur Lonend.'

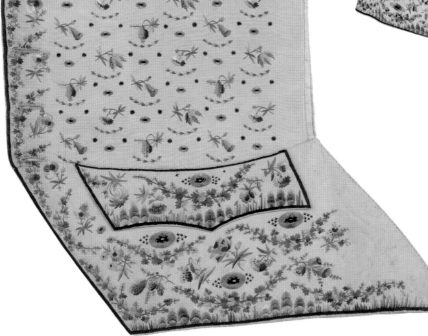

Sack-back gown, about 1765
Bought by Glasgow Museums, 1985
E.1986.62.5

Robe à la Française or sack-back gowns were informal loose-fitting
gowns initially, but became more structured during the mid-1800s
when they were worn as formal gowns. They were constructed with
a double-box pleat at the back from which the material draped to the
ground. On this example the edge has been caught up at the centre
back with a single button.

31

Sack-back gown, about 1765
Bought by Glasgow Museums, 1985
E.1986.62.4

Like the dress on the preceding page, this *robe à la Française* was worn by a relative of John Richardson, a wealthy cooper (barrel-maker) and later salmon merchant in Perth. Both gowns are decorated with serpentine lines of ruched silk robings down the front that reflect the artist William Hogarth's view that 'the beauty of intricacy lies in contriving winding shapes' (*Analysis of Beauty*, 1753).

'*...the beauty of intricacy lies in contriving winding shapes...*'

Jacket, 1780–81

Given by Mrs Anne D Houston, 1932
1932.51.o

The cut of this *caraco plissé* (pleated
jacket) is similar to those found
on the back of sack-back gowns.
It is made from cord-quilted linen
that has the pattern stitched in
two parallel lines through which
a narrow cord is threaded. It was
a popular choice of material for
outdoor summer clothing.

Polonaise gown, 1780–81
Given by Mrs Anne D Houston, 1932
1932.51.l–m

The three-quarter length overskirts of this gown are looped up into three sections at the back *à la Polonaise*. This style was named after Poland, which featured prominently in European news following its division by Russia, Prussia and Austria in 1772. It was worn by Mary Macdowall, who married George Houston of Johnstone Castle in 1779. The large size of the bodice in comparison to Mary's other surviving gowns suggests that it may have been worn while she was pregnant.

English gown

During the late 1700s a more informal style of dress known as the *robe à l'Anglaise* (English gown) became popular in Europe. The wide side panniers of mid-1700s gowns were replaced with a softer round shape over the hips created by wearing a padded bum roll.

English gowns had closed bodices at the front that did not require the addition of a triangular-shaped stomacher. This beautiful gown has an unusual style of closing. The two front panels are fitted by pulling the three pairs of ribbons that tie at the front to create horizontal ruching. This style makes use of the softer, draping quality of muslin which can be gathered easily. This is in contrast to the stiffer silks that had been fashionable for the majority of the 1700s, which were normally pleated.

Cotton calicos and lighter-weight muslins were very popular in the late 1700s. These fabrics were imported from India originally, but due to growing demand began to be manufactured in Britain. The delicate material on this gown is woven with white stripes, wood block-printed and hand-painted in five colours with the green created by over-printing yellow on blue.

English gown, about 1780–90
Given by Ernest Maclagan Wedderburn, 1940
E.1940.47.c

19th

Nineteenth-
century
costume

With the fall of the French monarchy in the 1790s the centre of fashion moved from Versailles to Paris, where it was led by Emperor Napoleon's first wife, Josephine. The Imperial court looked to the classical world for inspiration. The result was slim-lined, high-waisted gowns accessorized with soft, draping Kashmir shawls. But one historical revival led to others and the Neoclassical silhouette was slowly obscured by ruffs and frills that widened the shoulders and hem.

Menswear, which had been refined by the English trendsetter Beau Brummell's preference for dark coloured coats that emphasized good tailoring, became dandified during the reign of George IV in the 1820s. For a short period it was men who donned corsets in an effort to attain small waists.

When Queen Victoria succeeded to the throne in 1837, she and her husband, Prince Albert, were keen to support British industry, often making patriotic rather than purely fashionable choices – her wedding dress showcased Honiton lace from Devon. It was left to her contemporary, Empress Eugénie of France, to lead fashionable society, which she did with the assistance of a young Englishman, Charles Frederick Worth. Traditionally people purchased a length of fabric, which they took to a dressmaker to have made up into a garment. Worth was the first to design and make dresses for sale alongside the fabrics. When Worth reopened his business in 1871 after the Franco-Prussian war he became the first true couturier, showing his own label designs each season for clients to select from.

Key inventions such as sewing machines, aniline dyes and paper patterns helped revolutionize the fashion industry, allowing for the mass production of garments. Magazines with hand-coloured fashion prints spread the news of what was in and out of fashion and helped to fuel demand, which was met by the large warehouses and department stores that began to dominate the shopping streets of major cities.

'...for a period it was men who donned corsets...'

Muslin dress

Neoclassical dresses with high waistlines inspired by Ancient Greek and Roman statues were fashionable in the early 1800s. Finely-woven white cotton muslin was often used in imitation of the white marble of these sculptures.

The earliest muslins were manufactured by hand in India and imported by the East India Company. However, due to developments in the British textile industry it became possible to manufacture fine quality muslins in the United Kingdom to meet the growing demand for the fabric.

This gown is made from a jamdani-style muslin – a fine muslin with a woven design made in Bengal – woven by Brown, Sharp and Co., Paisley. The company was established as a silk gauze weaving company in 1753 and by the 1770s was producing a wide range of muslins. Paisley was a significant textile-producing town. As well as weaving, there were many associated bleaching, dyeing, printing and embroidery firms. The most successful long-term area of production was thread manufacturing, which became a major international industry by the end of the 1800s.

Dress in muslin by Brown, Sharp & Co., Paisley, about 1800
Bought by Glasgow Museums with the assistance of the Camphill Fund, 2013
E.2013.7

Dress, about 1837–40
Given by the Misses Robertson, 1954
E.1954.10.a

In the early 1800s there were improvements in dyeing and printing techniques that allowed mass-production of textiles. Together with the repeal of excise duty on printed textiles in 1831 this meant that the cost of colourfully-printed fabrics was reduced greatly. Consumption grew as a result, and light-weight, plain-weave woollen fabrics known as challis or *delaine* (from the French 'of wool') took colour particularly well and became a popular practical choice for day dresses.

Slippers by J Macneille, about 1830–40
Given by Miss Eunice G Murray, 1955
E.1955.86.v

This pair of evening shoes, known as slippers, is made with black silk satin uppers embroidered with flowers and leaves worked in satin stitch. The leather soles are cut in a symmetrical 'straight' shape with no difference between the left and right foot, but would have moulded to the individual feet when worn. The slippers were secured with the long, narrow ribbons that wrapped around the ankle and lower calf.

Riding habit, about 1838
Given by Mary MacEwan, 1974
E.1974.33.1

Smart, tailored habits in hard-wearing wool broadcloth were worn whilst riding. This one was worn by Janet Fraser of Dornoch, the second wife of Lewis Hoyes, a Scottish merchant with property in Grenada. The long voluminous skirt would have been arranged after Janet was seated on her side saddle, and pinned in place by her groom. Whilst it provided warmth and modesty, it could have become hazardous if she fell from her horse. By the end of 1800s the voluminous skirts of riding habits were replaced with new forms of apron-style safety skirts.

'…it could have become hazardous if she fell from her horse…'

Caledonian hunting coat with waistcoat, about 1840–41
Given by Mrs Anne D Houston, 1947
E.1947.49.d & .f

Crimson red wool broadcloth was
a popular choice for hunt uniforms in the
early 1800s. The silver buttons on this
hunting coat worn by George Houston
are etched with a slender fox jumping
over a thistle. They are the insignia
of the Royal Caledonian Hunt.
Formed in 1777 to improve the
quality of fox hunting, the hunt
gained its Royal title in 1824.
Unusually the club did not
maintain its own pack of hounds,
but organized hunts and races
throughout southern Scotland.

Dress, about 1855–60
Given by Robert Gray, 1948
E.1948.145

During the 1850s the fashionable
silhouette for women's dresses
was expanding outwards.
Tiered pagoda sleeves echo
the deep flounces on the skirts
that produced additional girth.
Underneath increasing numbers of
petticoats were added – as many
as fourteen in some instances.
These were eventually replaced
with the steel-framed cage-
crinoline, patented in 1856, that
allowed ladies' hemlines to grow
to even larger dimensions in the
mid-1860s.

Girl's dress by J Godsell & Co., London, about 1860
Given by Mrs RH Barclay, 1985
E.1985.135.1

Tartan, originally the regional cloth of the Highlands, became fashionable throughout British society in the mid-1800s. Traditionally woven in wool, it was increasingly made in silk for evening wear. Its popularity was due in part to Queen Victoria's purchase of the Balmoral estate in Aberdeenshire in 1852. A new larger castle was built for her family's private use, which was decorated with specially-commissioned tartans.

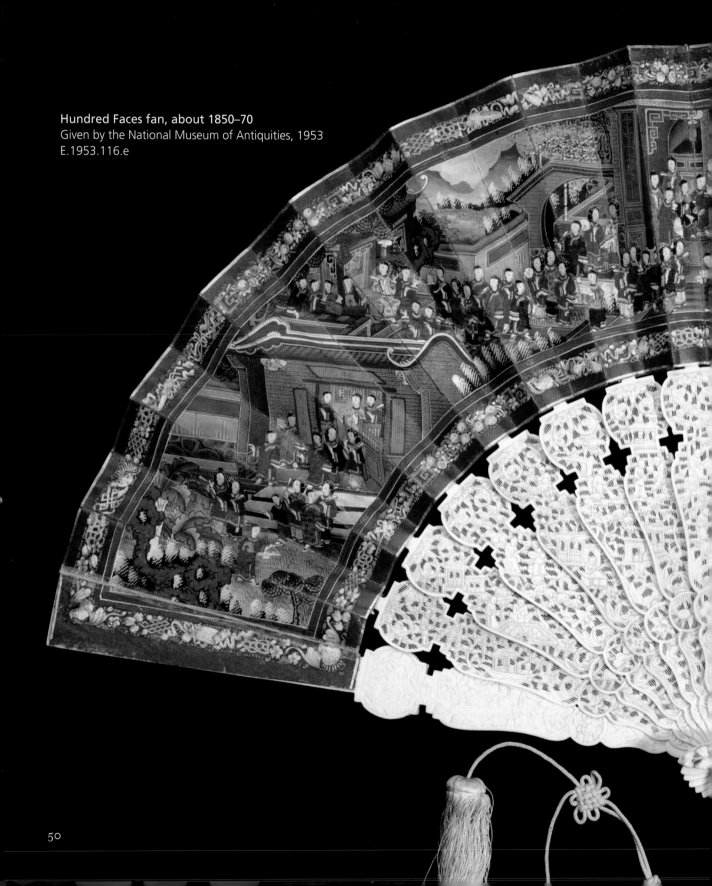

Hundred Faces fan, about 1850–70
Given by the National Museum of Antiquities, 1953
E.1953.116.e

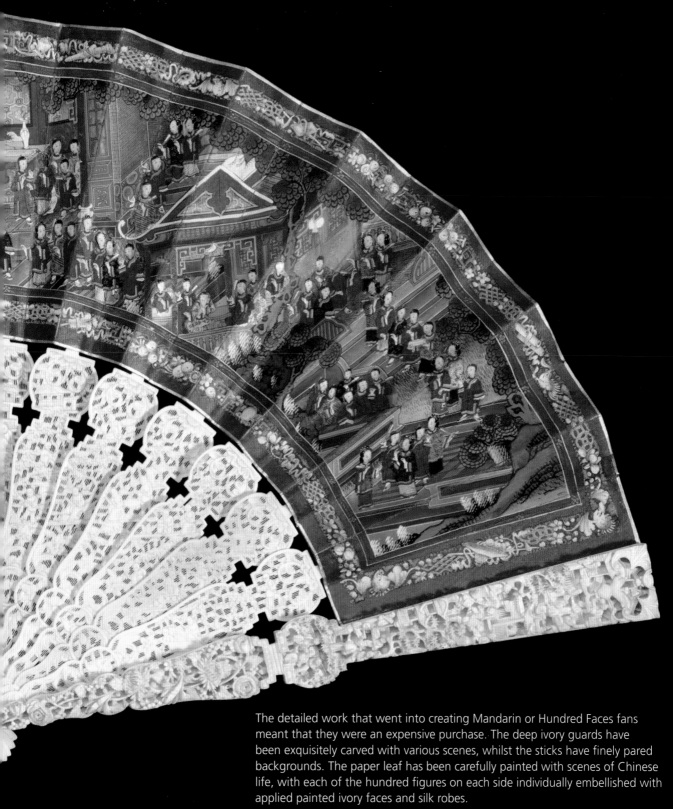

The detailed work that went into creating Mandarin or Hundred Faces fans meant that they were an expensive purchase. The deep ivory guards have been exquisitely carved with various scenes, whilst the sticks have finely pared backgrounds. The paper leaf has been carefully painted with scenes of Chinese life, with each of the hundred figures on each side individually embellished with applied painted ivory faces and silk robes.

Wedding dress by Miss Armour, Glasgow, 1878
Given by Miss Baird, 1953
E.1953.87.a

OBJECT IN FOCUS
Wedding dress

On 10 February 1840 Queen Victoria wore a cream silk dress at her wedding to Prince Albert instead of the traditional Robes of Estate and tissue (silver or gold fabric) gown normally worn by Royal brides. This nationally-publicized wedding helped to drive the tradition for well-to-do brides to marry in white, even if in practice this was often a shade of ivory or cream.

This wedding dress was made by Miss Armour, a dress and cloak maker. It is in the fashionable Princessline where the bodice panels are cut in one with the skirt. The style was created by Charles Frederick Worth, the first couturier, and named after Alexandra, Princess of Wales. The collar and cuffs are trimmed with blue forget-me-nots that represent true love – blue is traditionally the colour of fidelity.

This outfit was worn by Jessie Morrison Inglis at her wedding to the Reverend John Baird on 18 September 1878. Jessie was raised by her uncle, John Inglis, a wealthy Glaswegian shipbuilder. The couple had four children, including the television pioneer John Logie Baird.

Dress by Merlot Larchevêque, Paris, about 1880–81
Given by Dr MMP Jolly, 1974
E.1974.28.2

By the late 1800s Paris was the acknowledged centre of fashion, home to the first couturiers. Merlot Larchevêque was situated in a prime location on the Boulevard des Capucines, one of the four *grands boulevards*, opposite the Grand Hotel. The company advertised in British and American magazines, emphasizing that their staff spoke English. This dress, with its bead embellished bodice and over-skirt, is a wonderful example of fashionable black favoured by chic Parisian ladies in the 1880s.

Dress by R Simpson and Sons, Glasgow, about 1883
Given by Miss Dorothy Simpson, 1948
E.1948.144

R Simpson and Co. was originally founded as a shawl warehouse by Robert Simpson. It changed to 'and Sons' in 1851 after the next generation, James and Robert Kirk, joined the company. By the 1880s the firm had expanded into a five-floor department store on the corner of Jamaica and Argyle Streets, Glasgow. The Ladies' Department sold both fabrics and haberdashery, but also complete 'costumes, mantles and jackets'. This beautiful dress in warp-printed silk chine was worn by Robert Kirk Simpson's wife, Annie.

Dress by Simpson, Hunter and Young, Glasgow, about 1894
Given by Mrs E Wallace, 1973
E.1973.57.e

Simpson, Hunter and Young was founded in 1854 after the merger of three warehouses owned by Thomas Simpson, Andrew Hunter, and Alexander Young. Their premises at 59 Buchanan Street were in the heart of what was becoming the second largest city in the United Kingdom. The firm prided itself on following Parisian fashions closely, with this dress displaying the voluminous gigot or leg-of-mutton sleeves popular during the mid-1890s.

Dress by Madame Hayward, London, 1899
Bought by Glasgow Museums, 1988
E.1988.104.2

This fashionable two-piece walking dress was
made by Madame Hayward, a court dressmaker
with premises at 64 New Bond Street, London.
She made formal dresses for society ladies and
also provided the female costumes for several
theatre productions in the West End, London,
and Broadway, New York. This outfit was worn
as a going-away dress by Elizabeth Holms-
Kerr, the daughter of a wealthy Glaswegian
stockbroker, after her wedding to John Deans
Hope in March 1899.

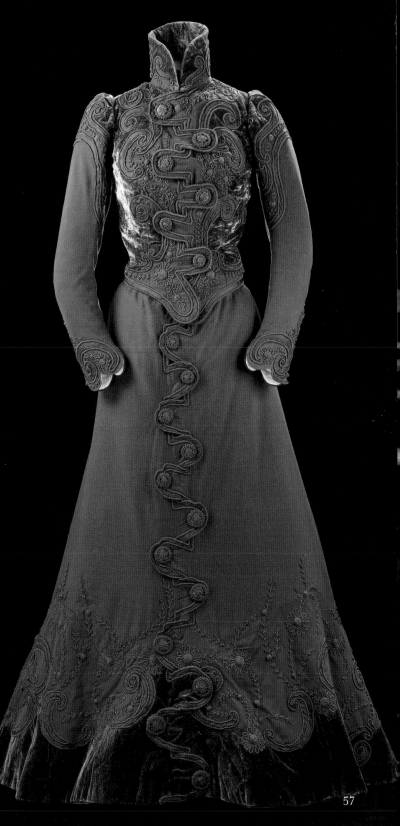

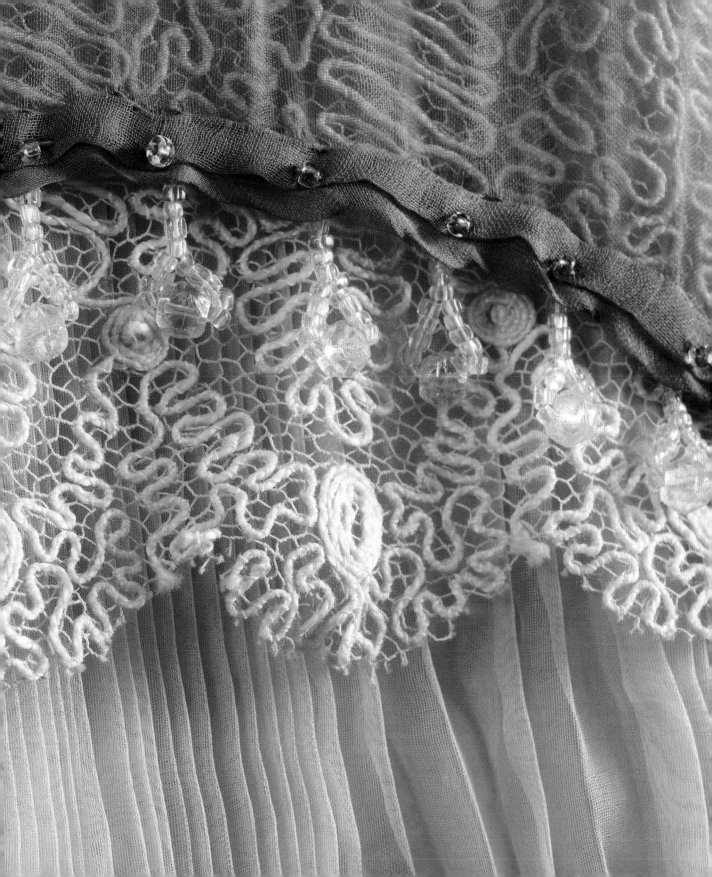

The Edwardian fashions of the early 1900s favoured pretty, feminine summer dresses and sumptuous evening gowns. Pastels were popular until Sergei Diaghilev introduced a Russian palette of bright colours that was echoed in the Middle Eastern and Oriental-inspired designs of French couturier Paul Poiret. However, women's bodies were constrained, first by the S-bend corset, and then by the hobble-skirt. It took World War I and the Suffrage movement to bring in a radical change in womenswear. Clothing became more practical, with shorter hemlines and less restrictive foundation garments, which were necessary as more women started to find employment.

The relaxation in dress codes continued into the 1920s. In Paris a new generation of designers, such as Gabrielle 'Coco' Chanel, introduced new youthful styles that were easier to wear. Increasingly people were spending more time undertaking leisure pursuits, which led to new markets emerging for specialist sportswear. Brand names began to emerge with fashion houses producing logos that were appeared on luxury ranges, such as perfume and stockings, sold to increasingly larger numbers of clientele.

World War II had a major impact on fashion in the 1940s. Many European governments introduced sumptuary laws that restricted the design and manufacture of clothing. It took a number of years for

'...Chanel introduced new youthful styles that were easier to wear...'

international trade links to start running again. When they did, it was not only textiles but also complete garments that began to be manufactured on a global scale, making use of cheaper labour.

The twentieth century saw major innovations in the creation of new synthetic fibres. During the 1960s fashion designers such as Paco Rabanne enjoyed working with space-age materials aimed at a market of young men and women with disposable incomes. Sub-cultures of fashion emerged, playing with how items were styled.

Collar by Jessie Rowat Newbery, about 1900
Given by Mr and Mrs F Lang, 1985
E.1985.162.4

Jessie Rowat was a student at The Glasgow School
of Art in 1884–88. She married Fra Newbery, the
Director of the School, in 1889. She subsequently
established embroidery classes there in 1894, and
went on to become one of the leading exponents of
the Glasgow Style. This collar, made from light green
linen with appliqué work, couched threads and beads,
demonstrates her strong linear designs.

Dress by Jessie Marion King, about 1918–22
Bought by Glasgow Museums, 1988
E.1988.150

Jessie Marion King studied at The Glasgow School of Art in 1892–99. She and her husband, the artist EA Taylor, moved to Paris in 1910. Whilst in France Jessie learnt batik, a form of wax-resist dyeing that originated in Java. Upon their return to Scotland in 1915 Jessie continued to work in this technique, making this dress for one of the daughters of her friend, Wendy Wood, the Scottish Independence campaigner.

Bathing costume, about 1900–10
Bought by Glasgow Museums, 2011
E.2011.13

Bathing became a popular leisure activity in the early 1900s. Appropriate clothing was developed that allowed Edwardians to dress decently whilst having the freedom of movement to swim. This combination bodice and bloomers has a matching wrap-around skirt for additional modesty. Nautical designs elements, such as the sailor-style collar, were particularly popular for bathing costumes during this period.

'...Nautical design elements... were particularly popular for bathing costumes...'

**Motoring coat by David Kemp and Son,
Glasgow, about 1910**
Given by Mrs SB Avery, 1975
E.1975.107.4

Early motor cars were open-topped and
required the driver and passengers to wear
suitable protective garments, such as a
motoring coat. This light-weight summer
example is made from a light cream wool
mix. It was made by David Kemp and
Son, who originally started as a shawl
manufacturer in 1832. However, they
expanded rapidly and moved to a
new five-storey premise at
37 Buchanan Street,
Glasgow, in 1854.

Dress by Copland & Lye, Glasgow, about 1912
Given by Miss Carslaw, 1974
E.1974.82.1

The Empire line of the early 1800s, with its raised
waistline and slim skirts, was reintroduced in 1908
by the young French designer, Paul Poiret. This
example was made a few years later by Copland &
Lye, which was founded by William Copland and
John Lye in 1873. It may have been influenced by
Mariano Fortuny y Madrazo's finely pleated silk
Delphos dresses, which were first made in 1907.

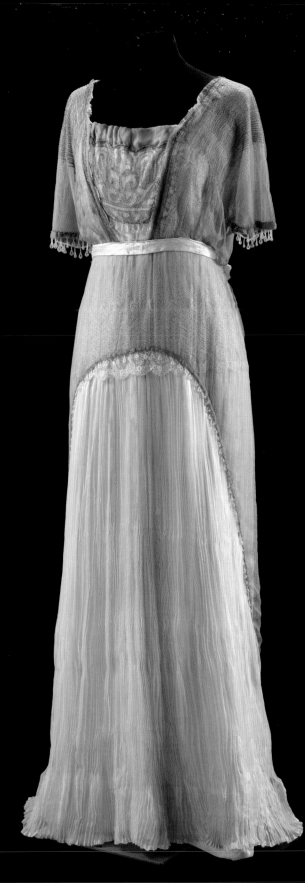

Pochoir print, George Barbier, from the *Journal des Dames et des Modes*, 10 April 1913
SP.2009.3.40

George Barbier was one of the most influential designers and illustrators in Paris in the early 1900s. He was commissioned to design theatre costumes as well as to produce fashion illustrations. His prints for the *Journal des Dames et des Modes* featured his own designs rather than depictions of couturiers' models. This allowed him complete artistic licence to create vibrant outfits whose colour and line would complement the background in his prints.

'Evening gown, flesh-coloured mousseline bodice, silk tunic embroidered in the style of the East India Company.'

1913   *Costumes Parisiens*   69

G. BARBIER
1913

Grande robe du soir, corsage de mousseline chair, tunique de soie brodée dans le goût de la "Compagnie des Indes".

Dress by Lanvin

Jeanne Lanvin trained originally as a milliner, opening a hat shop in Paris in 1890. When the clothes that she made for her daughter, Marguerite, received attention Lanvin expanded her business to include dresses. In 1909 she joined the Syndicate de Couture and became one of the leading couturiers in Paris.

One of Lanvin's early successes was the 'robes des style' which were based on mid-1700s gowns. They were cut with low waistlines and full skirts that often widened over the hips to imitate panniers. Elements of this cut are seen in this stunning red crêpe dress.

As well as being inspired by historical dress, fashion at this period was influenced by oriental designs, especially after Sergei Diaghilev's Ballet Russes performed their first season in Paris in 1909. Bright colours and linear surface patterns became popular. The design on this vibrant dress is worked in black and metal thread with ruched silk and net adding texture.

Dress by Jeanne Lanvin, Paris, about 1923
Bought by Glasgow Museums, 1978
E.1978.86

Dress by Marcher, 1949
Given by Miss McCutcheon, 1975
E.1975.118.2

Restrictions on the availability of goods
not only during but also after World War II
resulted in rationing and the utility scheme,
which prescribed the amount of material
and trimmings which could be used in a
garment. A range of slightly more luxurious
garments was created in the late 1940s.
These were labelled with a Double Eleven
logo – IIOII – signifying that they still met
government specifications.

Dress by Christian Dior, Paris, about 1950
Bought by Glasgow Museums, 1973
E.1973.16

Christian Dior's first collection, nick-named the 'New
Look' after the austere fashions of World War II, created
a sensation when it was launched in 1947 and propelled
the young couturier to international fame. The feminine
silhouette, as seen on this sumptuous evening dress with
its pinched-in waist and full skirt supported by a net
petticoat, dominated fashion for the next decade.

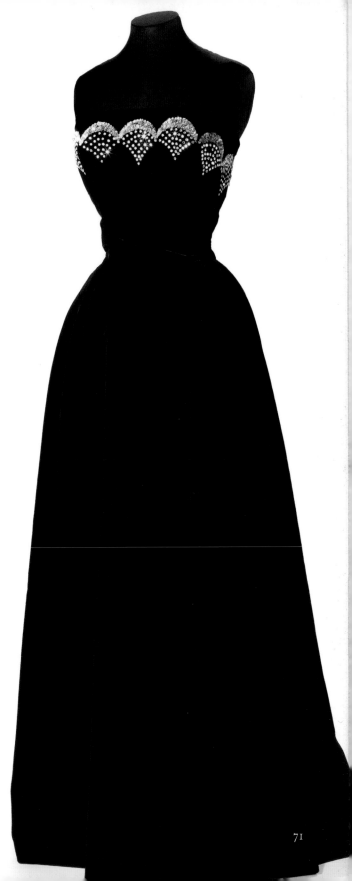

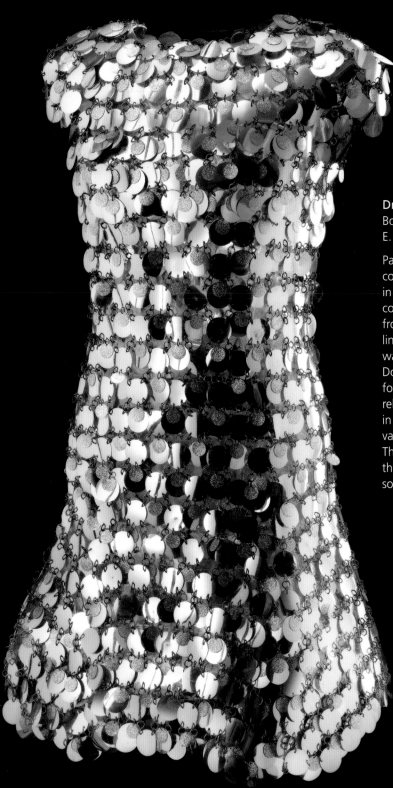

Dress by Paco Rabanne, Paris, 1966
Bought by Glasgow Museums, 1990
E.1990.6.15

Paco Rabanne launched his first
collection, 'Twelve Unwearable Dresses
in Contemporary Materials', in 1966. It
consisted of imitation mail dresses made
from Rhodoid cellulose acetate plastic disks
linked together with metal rings. This one
was worn by Audrey Hepburn in Stanley
Donen's film *Two For the Road* (1967), which
followed the first ten years of a couple's
relationship. Hepburn's evolving dress style
in the movie helps viewers identify the
various periods in the couple's relationship.
The Rabanne dress was worn at a party near
the end of the movie by an older and more
sophisticated version of the character.

'Island Paradise' dress by Hallmark, USA, about 1967–68
E.1976.9.1

Paper dresses were first introduced in America by the Scott Paper Company in 1966 as a marketing tool. Their huge popularity led to several other companies and fashion designers producing paper dresses. Hallmark, the American greetings card manufacturer, produced a wide range of paper dresses that were designed to be worn when hosting parties and co-ordinated with the company's ranges of colourful paper plates, napkins and tablecloths.

Outfit by John Bates, London, about 1972–73
Given by Marilyn Neil, 1987
E.1987.105.1

In 1959 John Bates created the Jean Varon label,
believing that a French name would have more
appeal than his own. The designs were aimed at
young women and included Diana Rigg's outfits
as Mrs Peel in the television series *The Avengers*.
John Bates established a more expensive, up-
market range of clothing under his own name
label in 1972.

Outfit by Pringle of Scotland for Daly's, Glasgow, about 1974–75
Given by Miss Agnes Gillies, 1986
E.1986.146.2

Pringle of Scotland was established by Robert Pringle in 1815 and is one of several companies based in Hawick in the Scottish Borders that specialize in manufacturing woollen garments. Initially the company made hosiery, but began making luxury pieces in cashmere in the late 1800s. This black cashmere two-piece outfit was made exclusively for Daly's, a Glasgow department store, which was taken over by House of Fraser in 1952, which continued to use the Daly's name until 1979.

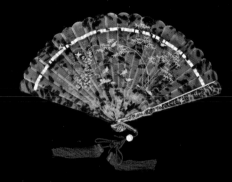

'Key inventions such as sewing machines,
aniline dyes and paper patterns helped
revolutionize the fashion industry...'

Rebecca Quinton
Glasgow Museums